GARLANDS OF GRACE

Garlands of Grace

An Anthology of
Great Christian Poetry

~

Selected and Introduced
by
REGIS MARTIN

IGNATIUS PRESS   SAN FRANCISCO

Cover art: J. B. L. Franquelin (17th c.).
Frontispiece of the Map of North America. Late 17th c.
Service Historique de la Marin, Vincennes, France.
Giraudon/Art Resource, N.Y.

Cover design by Riz Boncan Marsella

ISBN 0-89870-846-x
Library of Congress control number: 00-111221
Printed in the United States of America ∞

. . . people are exasperated by poetry which they
do not understand, and contemptuous of poetry
which they understand without effort . . .

T. S. Eliot

The rhetorician would deceive his neighbors,
The sentimentalist himself; while art
Is but a vision of reality.

W. B. Yeats

In

memory

of

the finest teacher I ever knew,

Fritz Wilhelmsen,

1923–1996,

who first awakened me to the

poetry of the transcendent

Contents

Introduction

Two themes, two polarities as it were, define the condition of man in a fallen world: that of the misery in which he is abjectly sunk and that of the grandeur to which he is nevertheless called. Gravity and grace. The downward pull of the one; the upward surge of the other. On one side, an impacted oppression of sin, depravity, and death; on the other, an exhilaration of grace, glory, and God. There, amid so many splendid, unending collisions, is a man's life to be found. And only in death does one at last arrive at such resolution as befits a being not meant for this world; indeed, a creature the total trajectory of whose being is intended to carry him breathcatchingly beyond this world.

But how exactly does one set about finding this point of highest resolution? It can hardly exist in man since that very finality with which he is most exaltingly inscribed makes no provision at all for so complete an inadequacy of native equipment. Yes, we may see the distant hills, but we are scarcely in a position to climb any of them. Fated thus to gaze upon the infinite stars even as he languishes in the nearest ditch, man remains (so Pascal reminds us) the middle point between nothing and everything. A sheer line of horizon betwixt time and eternity, and who among us is equal to the tension? At once anchored to flesh—bone, marrow and matter—our souls may at any moment be wafted into purest seraphic space. But, again, who can maintain so exquisite a balance? Who will untie the knot, releasing us from the coils in whose clutches we are so often caught? Only God, it seems, is able to reach right down to the very heart of our wretchedness, there to pry man loose for the journey home to Heaven. Surely it must be the most amazing sleight-of-hand, accomplished precisely amid the frightful events of His Son's Death, Descent, and Resurrection. We are thus enabled, in the words of the poet Donne which he addresses to God Himself,

> to find both Adams met in me;
> As the first Adam's sweat surrounds my face,
> May the second Adam's blood my soul embrace.

If Christ be then the point of sublimest resolution, His Body broken upon the wood of a Cross fashioned for our salvation, how vast and profound must be the wounds of this world! Who among us, I am saying, has not often felt that stabbing sense of contradiction between the ideals he professes and, alas, their shabby betrayal? So many lofty promises painfully mocked by abject performance. As T. S. Eliot puts it in "The Hollow Men":

> Between the idea
> And the reality
> Between the motion
> And the act
> Falls the shadow.

Yet we have it on faith that no shadow exists—no wound of sin so deep, nor the scar tissue of accumulated corruption so thick—to overmaster the power of the mercy of Christ.

> . . . for Christ plays in ten thousand places,
> Lovely in limbs, and lovely in eyes not his
> To the Father through the features of men's faces.
>
> — Gerard Manley Hopkins

How paltry our understanding of His Passion if we cannot see that, at the deepest level of divine love, we are delivered not only from our sin and squalor but even in the midst of such sin and squalor. When the form of God broke upon the wheel of death, Christ burst upon the world's body, His sacred humanity stretched to the uttermost limit of that universe God willed for Him to encompass and redeem. God's Word having long since entered into man, there can be nothing so daunting therein to frighten or distress Him now.

"In Christ," writes Hans Urs von Balthasar, "we can now contemplate the interpretation both of God and of man: the heart of God interpreted in the heart of Christ, the heart of man in its fall into inauthenticity and lostness caught up and restored . . . in this same heart on the cross." Within that ambit of humanity assumed by Christ—to sound the great theme of Recapitulation which Mother Church, in the writings of St. Irenaeus, deployed as a most adroit club with which to beat back the Gnostic onslaught—"He raises man from the ground to which he has fallen . . . and by giving the whole of man scope in Himself he also assumes man's death into Himself." Or, as the immortal Hopkins will remind us in his most exultant mode, to wit, "That

Nature Is a Heraclitean Fire and of the Comfort of the Resurrection'':

> In a flash, at a trumpet crash,
> I am all at once what Christ is, | since he was what
>   I am, and
> This Jack, joke, poor potsherd, | patch, matchwood,
>   immortal diamond,
>   Is immortal diamond.

Man is never, therefore, simply his natural self; he is always more than the sum of the parts nature or science can confidently count. As numberless saints, and sinners, will tell us, man is a being out of joint; wounded by the devil with the lesion of concupiscence, and by God's free wound of love. And there is a sense, I want now to insist, in which the truth of that shattering paradox finds its most vivid and sustained and unforgettable expression, crystallizing in forms of the most heightened beauty and pathos, in the work of the artist and the poet. It is he who remains the indispensable maker of images, whose task is to re-present simply and honestly, with all the force and cunning of language, this persisting, paradoxical reality. If there be more truth in poetry than in history, as Aristotle teaches, then we must attend to what the poets have to say. "Though in themselves of no help to the attainment of eternal life," concedes the philosopher Jacques Maritain, "art and poetry are more necessary than bread to the human race. They fit it for the life of the spirit."

The most perfect definition of poetry I think I have ever seen came from the pen of the most perfect poet I ever read, T. S. Eliot, the rhythms and sonorities of whose verse rise with seeming majestic ease high above the usual dreary cacophony of our world. "Poetry", he pronounced with mock-magisterial accent, "is a superior amusement." (It is also, he allowed, "a mug's game", concerning which not even the poet himself can be certain of the ultimate value of what he's written. In that case, the late Marianne Moore was right when, beginning a poem of her own, she writes: "I, too, dislike it: there are things that are important beyond all/ this fiddle./ Reading it, however, with a perfect contempt for it, one/ discovers in/ it after all, a place for the genuine.")

A superior amusement. Hmm. An arresting formulation, it captures nicely the distinctive quality, the stylish cachet as it were, of Eliot's own remarkable verse. Of course the man had distressingly little competition, ours being an age singularly impoverished in its expression. If you do not believe me, take a moment to peruse the standard titles festooning the poetry shelves of almost any bookstore across America: from sea to shining sea, the most benumbing, incomprehensible bilge masquerading as Art—from the sentimentalized inanities of Rod McKuen and Suzanne Sommers, to the X-rated effusions of Rod Stewart and Jim Morrison, rock stars whose music (I am told) is ever worse than their verse. If poetry, as many of us once believed in our first innocence, begins in wonder and delight and ends in wisdom, today's formula would have it all begin in wit-lessness and depravity and end in forms of wantonness still worse.

The selections that follow have all been chosen primarily because they communicate that sense of "superior amusement" which poetry at its best is meant to impart. They also (for the most part) rhyme, which seems to me an almost non-negotiable minimum to the making of a good poem. Was it Robert Frost who said, "Writing free verse is like playing tennis with the net down"? Observing this stricture, I should add, enabled me blessedly to omit most of the moderns. That and of course the limitations of copyright law, which provides a pretty high net of its own. In any case, while I do not presume to have plucked the fairest blooms of poesy, I do believe that I have seized upon a number of striking specimens that amount to a convincing cross-section of some of the best Christian devotional verse written during the past four centuries, poems which in fact please and delight.

And more. Because, like the Sacred Text on which the faithful exegete is asked to meditate, these poems serve to deepen and renew the sense of mystery, especially that immense and continuing mystery, as yet unsolved by secularist ideology, regarding man's place in the cosmos; those oscillating currents of grandeur and misery which characterize our lives right from the start. For all that we remain exiles from Eden—countless deposed kings and queens, to lay hold of the famous Pascalian image—in frantic search, therefore, of lost kingdoms, we have all been summoned, thanks be to Christ, to the unending glory of an eternal Kingdom, where neither moth nor rust can eat away at those imperishable things to which we've been called. May these few garlands strung thus modestly together help quicken that hunger for God which is the end of all true devotion. *Deo gratias.*

R. M.

SIR WALTER RALEIGH
(1552–1618)

Epitaph

Even such is Time, that takes in trust
Our youth, our joys, our all we have,
And pays us but with age and dust;
   Who in the dark and silent grave,
When we have wandered all our ways,
Shuts up the story of our days;
But from this earth, this grave, this dust,
My God shall raise me up, I trust.

ROBERT SOUTHWELL
(1561–1595)

The Burning Babe

As I in hoary winter's night
  Stood shivering in the snow,
Surprised I was with sudden heat
  Which made my heart to glow;
And lifting up a fearful eye
  To view what fire was near,
A pretty babe all burning bright
  Did in the air appear,
Who, scorchèd with excessive heat,
  Such floods of tears did shed
As though His floods should quench His flames
  Which with His fears were bred.
'Alas!' quoth He, 'but newly born,
  In fiery heats I fry,
Yet none approach to warm their hearts
  Or feel my fire but I.

'My faultless breast the furnace is,
    The fuel wounding thorns;
Love is the fire, and sighs the smoke,
    The ashes, shame and scorns.
'The fuel Justice layeth on
    And Mercy blows the coals,
The metal in the furnace wrought
    Are men's defilèd souls;
'For which, as now on fire I am
    To work them to their good,
So will I melt into a bath
    To wash them in my blood.'
With this He vanished out of sight
    And swiftly shrunk away,
And straight I callèd unto mind
    That it was Christmas day.

JOHN DONNE
(1573–1631)

Sonnets

vii

At the round earth's imagin'd corners, blow
Your trumpets, Angels, and arise, arise
From death, you numberless infinities
Of souls, and to your scatter'd bodies go,
All whom the flood did, and fire shall o'erthrow,
All whom war, dearth, age, agues, tyrannies,
Despair, law, chance, hath slain, and you whose eyes,
Shall behold God, and never taste death's woe.
But let them sleep, Lord, and me mourn a space,
For, if above all these, my sins abound,
'Tis late to ask abundance of Thy grace,
When we are there; here on this lowly ground,
Teach me how to repent; for that's as good
As if Thou hadst seal'd my pardon, with Thy blood.

Death be not proud, though some have callèd thee
Mighty and dreadful, for, thou art not so,
For, those, whom thou think'st, thou dost overthrow,
Die not, poor death, nor yet canst thou kill me.
From rest and sleep, which but thy pictures be,
Much pleasure, then from thee, much more must flow,
And soonest our best men with thee do go,
Rest of their bones, and soul's delivery.
Thou art slave to Fate, Chance, kings, and desperate men,
And dost with poison, war, and sickness dwell,
And poppy, or charms can make us sleep as well,
And better than thy stroke; why swell'st thou then?
One short sleep past, we wake eternally,
And death shall be no more; death, thou shalt die.

Batter my heart, three-person'd God; for you
As yet but knock, breathe, shine, and seek to mend;
That I may rise, and stand, o'erthrow me, and bend
Your force, to break, blow, burn and make me new.
I, like an usurp'd town, to another due,
Labour to admit you, but oh, to no end,
Reason your viceroy in me, we should defend,
But is captiv'd, and proves weak or untrue.
Yet dearly I love you, and would be loved fain,
But am betroth'd unto your enemy:
Divorce me, untie, or break that knot again,
Take me to you, imprison me, for I
Except you enthral me, never shall be free,
Nor ever chaste, except you ravish me.

A Hymn to God the Father

I

Wilt Thou forgive that sin where I begun,
  Which is my sin, though it were done before?
Wilt Thou forgive that sin, through which I run,
  And do run still: though still I do deplore?
    When Thou hast done, Thou hast not done,
      For I have more.

II

Wilt Thou forgive that sin by which I have won
  Others to sin? and, made my sin their door?
Wilt Thou forgive that sin which I did shun
  A year, or two: but wallowed in, a score?
    When Thou hast done, Thou hast not done,
      For I have more.

III

I have a sin of fear, that when I have spun
  My last thread, I shall perish on the shore;
Swear by Thyself, that at my death Thy Son
  Shall shine as He shines now, and heretofore;
    And, having done that, Thou hast done,
      I fear no more.

ROBERT HERRICK
(1591–1674)

His Litany to the Holy Spirit

In the hour of my distress,
When temptations me oppress,
And when I my sins confess,
    Sweet Spirit, comfort me!

When I lie within my bed,
Sick in heart and sick in head,
And with doubts discomforted,
    Sweet Spirit, comfort me!

When the house doth sigh and weep,
And the world is drown'd in sleep,
Yet mine eyes the watch do keep,
    Sweet Spirit, comfort me!

When the artless doctor sees
No one hope, but of his fees,
And his skill runs on the lees,
    Sweet Spirit, comfort me!

When his potion and his pill
Has, or none, or little skill,
Meet for nothing, but to kill;
    Sweet Spirit, comfort me!

When the passing bell doth toll,
And the Furies in a shoal
Come to fright a parting soul,
    Sweet Spirit, comfort me!

When the tapers now burn blue,
And the comforters are few,
And that number more than true,
  Sweet Spirit, comfort me!

When the priest his last hath prayed,
And I nod to what is said,
'Cause my speech is now decayed,
  Sweet Spirit, comfort me!

When, God knows, I'm toss'd about,
Either with despair, or doubt;
Yet before the glass be out,
  Sweet Spirit, comfort me!

When the tempter me pursu'th
With the sins of all my youth,
And half damns me with untruth,
  Sweet Spirit, comfort me!

When the flames and hellish cries
Fright mine ears, and fright mine eyes,
And all terrors me surprise,
  Sweet Spirit, comfort me!

When the Judgment is reveal'd,
And that open'd which was seal'd,
When to Thee I have appeal'd,
  Sweet Spirit, comfort me!

FRANCIS QUARLES
(1592–1644)

On Death

Why should we not, as well, desire death,
As sleep? No difference, but a little breath;
'Tis all but rest; 'tis all but a releasing
Our tired limbs; why then not alike pleasing?
Being burthened with the sorrows of the day,
We wish for night; which, being come, we lay
Our bodies down; yet when our very breath
Is irksome to us, we're afraid of death:
Our sleep is oft accompanied with frights,
Distracting dreams and dangers of the nights;
When in the sheets of death, our bodies sure
From all such evils, and we sleep secure:
What matter, down, or earth? what boots it whether?
Alas, our body's sensible of neither:
Things that are senseless, feel nor pains nor ease;
Tell me; and why not worms as well as fleas?
In sleep, we know not whether our closed eyes
Shall ever wake; from death we're sure to rise:
Aye, but 'tis long first; O, is that our fears?
Dare we trust God for nights? and not for years?

On Our Saviour's Passion

The earth did tremble; and heaven's closed eye
Was loath to see the Lord of Glory die:
The skies were clad in mourning, and the Spheres
Forgot their harmony; the clouds dropped tears;
Th' ambitious dead arose to give him room;
And every grave did gape to be His tomb;
Th' affrighted heavens sent down elegious thunder;
The world's foundation loosed, to lose their founder;
Th' impatient temple rent her veil in two,
To teach our hearts what our sad hearts should do:
Shall senseless things do this, and shall not I
Melt one poor drop to see my Saviour die?
Drill forth my tears; and trickle one by one,
Till you have pierced this heart of mine, this stone.

GEORGE HERBERT
(1593–1633)

Redemption

Having been tenant long to a rich Lord,
   Not thriving, I resolved to be bold,
   And make a suit unto him, to afford
A new small-rented lease, and cancell th' old.
In heaven at his manour I him sought:
   They told me there, that he was lately gone
   About some land, which he had dearly bought
Long since on earth, to take possession.
I straight return'd, and knowing his great birth,
   Sought him accordingly in great resorts;
   In cities, theatres, gardens, parks, and courts:
At length I heard a ragged noise and mirth
   Of thieves and murderers: there I him espied,
   Who straight, *Your suit is granted*, said, and died.

The Pulley

When God at first made man,
Having a glass of blessings standing by—
Let us (said He) pour on him all we can:
Let the world's riches, which dispersèd lie,
　　Contract into a span.

So strength first made a way,
Then beauty flow'd, then wisdom, honour, pleasure:
When almost all was out, God made a stay,
Perceiving that alone of all His treasure
　　Rest in the bottom lay.

For if I should (said He)
Bestow this jewel also on My creature,
He would adore My gifts instead of Me,
And rest in Nature, not the God of Nature:
　　So both should losers be.

Yet let him keep the rest,
But keep them with repining restlessness;
Let him be rich and weary, that at least,
If goodness lead him not, yet weariness
　　May toss him to My breast.

Love (III)

Love bade me welcome: yet my soul drew back,
    Guilty of dust and sin.
But quick-eyed Love, observing me grow slack
    From my first entrance in,
Drew nearer to me, sweetly questioning,
    If I lacked anything.

A guest, I answered, worthy to be here:
    Love said, You shall be he.
I the unkind, ungrateful? Ah my dear,
    I cannot look on thee.
Love took my hand, and smiling did reply,
    Who made the eyes but I?

Truth Lord, but I have marred them: let my shame
    Go where it doth deserve.
And know you not, says Love, who bore the blame?
    My dear, then I will serve.
You must sit down, says Love, and taste my meat:
    So I did sit and eat.

ANNE BRADSTREET
(1612?–1672)

Before the Birth of One of Her Children

All things within this fading world hath end,
Adversity doth still our joys attend;
No ties so strong, no friends so dear and sweet,
But with death's parting blow is sure to meet.
The sentence past is most irrevocable,
A common thing, yet oh inevitable.
How soon, my Dear, death may my steps attend,
How soon't may be thy Lot to lose thy friend,
We are both ignorant, yet love bids me
These farewell lines to recommend to thee,
That when that knot's untied that made us one,
I may seem thine, who in effect am none.
And if I see not half my dayes that's due,
What nature would, God grant to yours and you;
The many faults that well you know I have
Let be interr'd in my oblivious grave;
If any worth or virtue were in me,
Let that live freshly in thy memory
And when thou feel'st no grief, as I no harms,
Yet love thy dead, who long lay in thine arms.
And when thy loss shall be repaid with gains
Look to my little babes[,] my dear remains.
And if thou love thyself, or loved'st me[,]
These O protect from step Dames injury.

34

And if chance to thine eyes shall bring this verse,
With some sad sighs honour my absent Herse;
And kiss this paper for thy loves dear sake,
Who with salt tears this last Farewel did take.

RICHARD CRASHAW
(1613?–1649)

Divine Love

Lord, when the sense of Thy sweet grace
Sends up my soul to seek Thy face,
Thy blessed eyes breed such desire,
I die in love's delicious Fire.
  O Love, I am thy Sacrifice.
Be still triumphant, blessed eyes.
Still shine on me, fair suns! that I
Still may behold, though still I die.

Though still I die, I live again;
Still longing so to be still slain,
So gainful is such loss of breath.
I die even in desire of death.
  Still live in me this loving strife
Of living Death and dying Life.
For while Thou sweetly slayest me,
Dead to myself I live in Thee.

An Epitaph upon Husband and Wife
Who died and were buried together.

To these whom Death again did wed
This Grave's the second Marriage-Bed.
For though the hand of Fate could force
'Twixt Soul and body a Divorce,
It could not sever Man and Wife,
Because they both lived but one Life.
Peace, good Reader, do not weep;
Peace, the lovers are asleep.
They, sweet Turtles, folded lie
In the last knot that love could tie.
Let them sleep, let them sleep on,
Till the stormy night be gone,
And th' eternal morrow dawn;
Then the Curtains will be drawn,
And they wake into a Light
Whose day shall never sleep in Night.

THOMAS TRAHERNE
(1637–1674)

The Bible

That! That! There I was told
That I *the Son of God* am made,
His Image. O Divine! And that fine Gold,
  With all the Joys that here do fade,
Are but a Toy, compared to the Bliss
Which Heav'nly, God-like, and Eternal is.
  That We on earth are Kings;
And, tho we're cloath'd with mortal Skin,
Are Inward Cherubims; have Angels Wings;
  Affections, Thoughts, and Minds within,
Can soar through all the Coasts of Heav'n and Earth;
And shall be sated with Celestial Mirth.

ISAAC WATTS
(1674–1748)

Crucifixion to the World by the Cross of Christ
(*Galatians 6:14*)

When I survey the wondrous Cross
On which the Prince of Glory died,
My richest gain I count but loss,
And pour contempt on all my pride.

Forbid it, Lord, that I should boast
Save in the death of Christ, my God;
All the vain things that charm me most,
I sacrifice them to His blood.

See from His Head, His Hands, His Feet,
Sorrow and love flow mingled down;
Did e'er such love and sorrow meet?
Or thorns compose so rich a crown?

His dying crimson like a robe
Spreads o'er His body on the Tree,
Then am I dead to all the globe,
And all the globe is dead to me.

Were the whole realm of nature mine,
That were an offering far too small;
Love so amazing, so Divine,
Demands my soul, my life, my all.

To Christ, Who won for sinners grace
By bitter grief and anguish sore,
Be praise from all the ransom'd race
For ever and for evermore.

WILLIAM COWPER
(1731–1800)

Walking with God

Oh! for a closer walk with God,
　　A calm and heavenly frame;
A light to shine upon the road
　　That leads me to the Lamb!

Where is the blessedness I knew
　　When first I saw the Lord?
Where is the soul-refreshing view
　　Of Jesus and his word?

What peaceful hours I once enjoyed!
　　How sweet their memory still!
But they have left an aching void
　　The world can never fill.

Return, O holy Dove, return,
　　Sweet messenger of rest;
I hate the sins that made thee mourn,
　　And drove thee from my breast.

The dearest idol I have know,
　　Whate'er that idol be,
Help me to tear it from thy throne,
　　And worship only Thee.

So shall my walk be close with God,
　　Calm and serene my frame;
So purer light shall mark the road
　　That leads me to the Lamb.

WILLIAM BLAKE
(1757–1827)

The Divine Image

To Mercy Pity Peace and Love,
All pray in their distress:
And to these virtues of delight
Return their thankfulness.

For Mercy Pity Peace and Love,
Is God our father dear:
And Mercy Pity Peace and Love,
Is Man his child and care.

For Mercy has a human heart
Pity, a human face:
And Love, the human form divine,
And Peace, the human dress.

Then every man of every clime,
That prays in his distress,
Prays to the human form divine
Love Mercy Pity Peace.

And all must love the human form,
In heathen, turk or jew.
Where Mercy, Love & Pity dwell
There God is dwelling too.

Holy Thursday

Twas on a Holy Thursday their innocent faces clean
The children walking two & two in red & blue & green
Grey headed beadles walkd before with wands as white
as snow
Till into the high dome of Pauls they like Thames waters
flow

O what a multitude they seemd these flowers of London
town
Seated in companies they sit with radiance all their own
The hum of multitudes was there but multitudes of
lambs
Thousands of little boys & girls raising their innocent
hands

Now like a mighty wind they raise to heaven the voice
of song
Or like harmonious thunderings the seats of heaven
among
Beneath them sit the aged men wise guardians of the
poor
Then cherish pity, lest you drive an angel from your
door

WILLIAM WORDSWORTH
(1770–1850)

The Virgin

Mother! Whose virgin bosom was uncrost
  With the least shade of thought to sin allied;
  Woman! Above all women glorified,
Our tainted nature's solitary boast;
Purer than foam on central ocean tost;
  Brighter than eastern skies at daybreak strewn
  With fancied roses, than the unblemished moon
Before her wane begins on heaven's blue coast;

Thy image falls to earth. Yet some, I ween,
  Not unforgiven, the suppliant knee might bend
  As to a visible power, in which did blend
    All that was mixed and reconciled in thee
    Of mother's love with maiden purity,
Of high with low, celestial with terrene.

HENRY FRANCIS LYTE
(1793–1847)

Abide with Me

Abide with me! fast falls the eventide;
The darkness deepens: Lord, with me abide!
When other helpers fail, and comforts flee,
Help of the helpless, O abide with me!

I need Thy presence every passing hour:
What but Thy grace can foil the tempter's power?
Who like Thyself my guide and stay can be?
Through cloud and sunshine, O abide with me!

Swift to its close ebbs out life's little day;
Earth's joys grow dim, its glories pass away;
Change and decay in all around I see:
O Thou who changest not, abide with me!

I fear no foe, with Thee at hand to bless:
Ills have no weight, and tears no bitterness:
Where is death's sting? where, grave, the victory?
I triumph still, if Thou abide with me!

Hold Thou Thy cross before my closing eyes;
Shine through the gloom and point me to the skies;
Heav'n's morning breaks, and earth's vain shadows flee
In life, in death, O Lord, abide with me!

JOHN HENRY CARDINAL NEWMAN
(1801–1890)

Praise to the Holiest in the Height
(*From* The Dream of Gerontius)

Praise to the Holiest in the height,
   And in the depth be praise:
In all His words most wonderful;
   Most sure in all His ways.

O loving wisdom of our God!
   When all was sin and shame,
A second Adam to the fight
   And to the rescue came.

O wisest love! that flesh and blood,
   Which did in Adam fail,
Should strive afresh against the foe,
   Should strive and should prevail;

And that a higher gift than grace
   Should flesh and blood refine,
God's Presence and His very self,
   And Essence all-divine.

O generous love! that He who smote
   In man for man the foe,
The double agony in man
   For man should undergo;

And in the garden secretly,
   And on the cross on high,
Should teach His brethren and inspire
   To suffer and to die.

The Pillar of the Cloud

Lead, kindly Light, amid the encircling gloom;
    Lead Thou me on!
The night is dark, and I am far from home—
    Lead Thou me on!
Keep Thou my feet: I do not ask to see
The distant scene—one step enough for me.

I was not ever thus, nor pray'd that Thou
    Shouldst lead me on.
I loved to choose and see my path, but now
    Lead Thou me on!
I loved the garish day, and, spite of fears,
Pride ruled my will; remember not past years.

So long Thy power hath blest me, sure it still
    Will lead me on
O'er moor and fen, o'er crag and torrent, till
    The night is gone,
And in the morn those angel faces smile
Which I have loved long since, and lost awhile.

The Sign of the Cross

Whene'er across the sinful flesh of mine
    I draw the Holy Sign,
All good thoughts stir within me, and renew
    Their slumbering strength divine;
Till there springs up a courage high and true
    To suffer and to do.

And who shall say, but hateful spirits around,
    For their brief hour unbound,
Shudder to see, and wail their overthrow?
    While on far heathen ground
Some lonely Saint hails the fresh odour, though
    Its source he cannot know.

HENRY WADSWORTH LONGFELLOW
(1807–1882)

Dante

Oft have I seen at some cathedral door
   A labourer, pausing in the dust and heat
   Lay down his burden, and with reverent feet
   Enter, and cross himself, and on the floor
Kneel to repeat his paternoster o'er;
   Far off the noises of the world retreat;
   The loud vociferations of the street
   Become an undistinguishable roar.
So, as I enter here from day to day,
   And leave my burden at this minster gate,
   Kneeling in prayer, and not ashamed to pray,
The tumult of the time disconsolate
   To inarticulate murmurs dies away,
   While the eternal ages watch and wait.

ALFRED LORD TENNYSON
(1809–1882)

Crossing the Bar

Sunset and evening star,
  And one clear call for me!
And may there be no moaning of the bar,
  When I put out to sea,

But such a tide as moving seems asleep,
  Too full for sound and foam,
When that which drew from out the boundless deep
  Turns again home.

Twilight and evening bell,
  And after that the dark!
And may there be no sadness of farewell,
  When I embark;

For though from out our bourne of Time and Place
  The flood may bear me far,
I hope to see my Pilot face to face
  When I have crost the bar.

MATTHEW ARNOLD
(1822–1888)

Dover Beach

The sea is calm tonight,
The tide is full, the moon lies fair
Upon the straits;—on the French coast the light
Gleams and is gone; the cliffs of England stand,
Glimmering and vast, out in the tranquil bay.
Come to the window, sweet is the night-air!
Only, from the long line of spray
Where the sea meets the moon-blanched land,
Listen! you hear the grating roar
Of pebbles which the waves draw back, and fling,
At their return, up the high strand,
Begin, and cease, and then again begin,
With tremulous cadences slow, and bring
The eternal note of sadness in.

Sophocles long ago
Heard it on the Ægæan, and it brought
Into his mind the turbid ebb and flow
Of human misery; we
Find also in the sound a thought,
Hearing it by this distant northern sea.

The Sea of Faith
Was once, too, at the full, and round earth's shore
Lay like the folds of a bright girdle furled.
But now I only hear
Its melancholy, long, withdrawing roar,
Retreating, to the breath
Of the night-wind, down the vast edges drear
And naked shingles of the world.

Ah, love, let us be true
To one another! for the world, which seems
To lie before us like a land of dreams,
So various, so beautiful, so new,
Hath really neither joy, nor love, nor light,
Nor certitude, nor peace, nor help for pain;
And we are here as on a darkling plain
Swept with confused alarms of struggle and flight,
Where ignorant armies clash by night.

COVENTRY PATMORE
(1823–1896)

The Toys

My little Son, who look'd from thoughtful eyes
And moved and spoke in quiet grown-up wise,
Having my law the seventh time disobey'd,
I struck him, and dismiss'd
With hard words and unkiss'd,
—His mother, who was patient, being dead.
Then, fearing lest his grief should hinder sleep,
I visited his bed,
But found him slumbering deep,
With darken'd eyelids, and their lashes yet
From his late sobbing wet.
And I, with moan,
Kissing away his tears, left others of my own;
For, on a table drawn beside his head,
He had put, within his reach,
A box of counters and a red-vein'd stone,
A piece of glass abraded by the beach.
And six or seven shells,
A bottle with bluebells,
And two French copper coins, ranged there with careful
    art,
To comfort his sad heart.
So when that night I pray'd
To God, I wept, and said:
Ah, when at last we lie with trancèd breath,

Not vexing Thee in death,
And Thou rememberest of what toys
We made our joys,
How weakly understood
Thy great commanded good,
Then, fatherly not less
Than I whom Thou hast moulded from the clay,
Thou'lt leave Thy wrath, and say,
'I will be sorry for their childishness.'

GEORGE MACDONALD
(1824–1905)

The Sweeper of the Floor

Methought that in a solemn church I stood.
Its marble acres, worn with knees and feet,
Lay spread from door to door, from street to street.
Midway the form hung high upon the rood
Of Him who gave His life to be our good;
Beyond, priests flitted, bowed, murmured meet
Among the candles shining still and sweet.
Men came and went, and worshipped as they could;
And still their dust a woman with her broom,
Bowed to her work, kept sweeping to the door.
Then saw I slow through all the pillared gloom
Across the church a silent figure come.
"Daughter," it said, "Thou sweepest well my floor!"
"It is the Lord!" I cried, and saw no more.

Obedience

I said, "Let me walk in the fields."
  He said, "No, walk in the town."
I said, "There are no flowers there."
  He said, "No flowers, but a crown."

I said, "But the skies are black;
  There is nothing but noise and din."
And He wept as He sent me back;
  "There is more", he said; "There is sin."

I said, "But the air is thick,
　And fogs are veiling the sun."
He answered, "Yet souls are sick,
　And souls in the dark undone."

I said, "I shall miss the light,
　And friends will miss me, they say."
He answered, "Choose to-night
　If *I* am to miss you, or they."

I pleaded for time to be given.
　He said, "Is it hard to decide?
It will not seem hard in heaven
　To have followed the steps of your Guide."

I cast one look at the fields,
　Then set my face to the town;
He said, "My child, do you yield?
　Will you leave the flowers for the crown?"

Then into His hand went mine,
　And into my heart came He;
And I walk in a light divine
　The path I had feared to see.

Lost and Found

I missed him when the sun began to bend;
I found him not when I had lost his rim;
With many tears I went in search of him,
Climbing high mountains which did still ascend,
And gave me echoes when I called my friend;
Through cities vast and charnel-houses grim,
And high cathedrals where the light was dim,
Through books and arts and works without an end,
But found him not—the friend whom I had lost.
And yet I found him—as I found the lark,
A sound in fields I heard but could not mark;
I found him nearest when I missed him most;
I found him in my heart, a life in frost,
A light I knew not till my soul was dark.

EMILY DICKINSON
(1830–1886)

If My Bark Sink

If my bark sink
'Tis to another sea.
Mortality's ground floor
Is immortality.

I Never Saw a Moor

I never saw a moor,
I never saw the sea;
Yet know I how the heather looks,
And what a wave must be.

I never spoke with God,
Nor visited in heaven;
Yet certain am I of the spot
As if the chart were given.

CHRISTINA G. ROSSETTI
(1830–1894)

Uphill

Does the road wind uphill all the way?
  Yes, to the very end.
Will the day's journey take the whole long day?
  From morn to night, my friend.

But is there for the night a resting-place?
  A roof for when the slow, dark hours begin.
May not the darkness hide it from my face?
  You cannot miss that inn.

Shall I meet other wayfarers at night?
  Those who have gone before.
Then must I knock, or call when just in sight?
  They will not keep you waiting at that door.

Shall I find comfort, travel-sore and weak?
  Of labour you shall find the sum.
Will there be beds for me and all who seek?
  Yea, beds for all who come.

Are Ye Not Much Better Than They?

The twig sprouteth,
The moth outeth,
The plant springeth,
The bird singeth:
Tho' little we sing today
Yet are we better than they;
Tho' growing with scarce a showing,
Yet, please God, we are growing.

The twig teacheth,
The moth preacheth,
The plant vaunteth,
The bird chanteth,
God's mercy overflowing,
Merciful past man's knowing,
Please God to keep us growing
Till the awful day of mowing.

The Voice of My Beloved

Once I ached for thy dear sake:
Wilt thou cause Me now to ache?
Once I bled for thee in pain:
Wilt thou rend My Heart again?
Crown of thorns and shameful tree.
Bitter death I bore for thee,
Bore My Cross to carry thee,
And wilt thou have nought of Me?

ABRAM J. RYAN
(1839–1886)

A Child's Wish

I wish I were the little key
   That locks Love's Captive in,
And lets Him out to go and free
   A sinful heart from sin.

I wish I were the little bell
   That tinkles for the Host
When God comes down each day to dwell
   With hearts He loves the most.

I wish I were the chalice fair
   That holds the Blood of Love,
When every flash lights holy prayer
   Upon its way above.

I wish I were the little flower
   So near the Host's sweet face,
Or like the light that half an hour
   Burned on the shrine of grace.

I wish I were the altar where
   As on His mother's breast
Christ nestles, like a child, fore'er
   In Eucharistic rest.

But oh, my God, I wish the most
   That my poor heart may be
A home all holy for each Host
   That comes in love to me.

THOMAS HARDY
(1839–1928)

The Choirmaster's Burial

He often would ask us
That, when he died,
After playing so many
To their last rest,
If out of us any
Should here abide,
And it would not task us,
We would with our lutes
Play over him
By his grave-brim
The psalm he liked best—
The one whose sense suits
'Mount Ephraim'—
And perhaps we should seem
To him, in Death's dream,
Like the seraphim.

As soon as I knew
That his spirit was gone
I thought this his due,
And spoke thereupon.
'I think,' said the vicar,
'A read service quicker
Than viols out-of-doors
In these frosts and hoars.

That old-fashioned way
Requires a fine day,
And it seems to me
It had better not be.'

Hence, that afternoon,
Though never knew he
That his wish could not be,
To get through it faster
They buried the master
Without any tune.
But 'twas said that, when
At the dead of next night
The vicar looked out,
There struck on his ken
Thronged roundabout,
Where the frost was graying
The headstoned grass,
A band all in white
Like the saints in church-glass,
Singing and playing
The ancient stave
By the choirmaster's grave.

Such the tenor man told
When he had grown old.

GERARD MANLEY HOPKINS
(1844–1889)

God's Grandeur

The world is charged with the grandeur of God.
   It will flame out, like shining from shook foil;
   It gathers to a greatness, like the ooze of oil
Crushed. Why do men then now not reck his rod?
Generations have trod, have trod, have trod;
   And all is seared with trade; bleared, smeared with
      toil;
   And wears man's smudge and shares man's smell: the
      soil
Is bare now, nor can foot feel, being shod.

And for all this, nature is never spent;
   There lives the dearest freshness deep down things;
And though the last lights off the black West went
   Oh, morning, at the brown brink eastward, springs—
Because the Holy Ghost over the bent
   World broods with warm breast and with ah! bright
      wings.

The Starlight Night

Look at the stars! look, look up at the skies!
   O look at all the fire-folk sitting in the air!
   The bright boroughs, the circle-citadels there!
Down in dim woods the diamond delves! the elves'-eyes!

The grey lawns cold where gold, where quickgold lies!
  Wind-beat whitebeam! airy abeles set on a flare!
  Flake-doves sent floating forth at a farmyard scare!
Ah well! it is all a purchase, all is a prize.

Buy then! bid then!—What?—Prayer, patience, alms,
    vows.
Look, look: a May-mess, like on orchard boughs!
  Look! March-bloom, like on mealed-with-yellow
    sallows!
These are indeed the barn; withindoors house
The shocks. This piece-bright paling shuts the spouse
  Christ home, Christ and his mother and all his
    hallows.

Pied Beauty

Glory be to God for dappled things—
  For skies of couple-colour as a brinded cow;
    For rose-moles all in stipple upon trout that swim;
Fresh-firecoal chestnut-falls; finches' wings;
  Landscape plotted and pieced—fold, fallow, and
    plough;
    And áll trádes, their gear and tackle and trim.

All things counter, original, spare, strange;
  Whatever is fickle, freckled (who knows how?)
    With swift, slow; sweet, sour; adazzle, dim;
He fathers-forth whose beauty is past change:
                    Praise him.

Spring

Nothing is so beautiful as spring—
   When weeds, in wheels, shoot long and lovely and
      lush;
   Thrush's eggs look little low heavens, and thrush
Through the echoing timber does so rinse and wring
The ear, it strikes like lightnings to hear him sing;
   The glassy peartree leaves and blooms, they brush
   The descending blue; that blue is all in a rush
With richness; the racing lambs too have fair their fling.

What is all this juice and all this joy?
   A strain of the earth's sweet being in the beginning
In Eden garden.—Have, get, before it cloy,
   Before it cloud, Christ, lord, and sour with sinning,
Innocent mind and Mayday in girl and boy,
   Most, O maid's child, thy choice and worthy the
      winning.

Spring and Fall:

to a young child

Márgarét, are you gríeving
Over Goldengrove unleaving?
Leáves, líke the things of man, you
With your fresh thoughts care for, can you?
Áh! ás the heart grows older
It will come to such sights colder
By and by, nor spare a sigh
Though worlds of wanwood leafmeal lie;

And yet you will weep and know why.
Now no matter, child, the name:
Sórrow's springs áre the same.
Nor mouth had, no nor mind, expressed
What heart heard of, ghost guessed:
It ís the blight man was born for,
It is Margaret you mourn for.

In honour of St. Alphonsus Rodriguez
Laybrother of the Society of Jesus

Honour is flashed off exploit, so we say;
And those strokes once that gashed flesh or galled shield
Should tongue that time now, trumpet now that field,
And, on the fighter, forge his glorious day.
On Christ they do and on the martyr may;
But be the war within, the brand we wield
Unseen, the heroic breast not outward-steeled,
Earth hears no hurtle then from fiercest fray.

 Yet God (that hews mountain and continent,
Earth, all, out; who, with trickling increment,
Veins violets and tall trees makes more and more)
Could crowd career with conquest while there went
Those years and years by of world without event
That in Majorca Alfonso watched the door.

'Thou Art Indeed Just, Lord, If I Contend'

*Justus quidem tu es, Domine, si disputem tecum: verumtamen
justa loquar ad te: Quare via impiorum prosperatur? &c.*

Thou art indeed just, Lord, if I contend
With thee; but, sir, so what I plead is just.
Why do sinners' ways prosper? and why must
Disappointment all I endeavour end?
    Wert thou my enemy, O thou my friend,
How wouldst thou worse, I wonder, than thou dost
Defeat, thwart me? Oh, the sots and thralls of lust
Do in spare hours more thrive than I that spend,
Sir, life upon thy cause. See, banks and brakes
Now, leavèd how thick! lacèd they are again
With fretty chervil, look, and fresh wind shakes
Them; birds build—but not I build; no, but strain,
Time's eunuch, and not breed one work that wakes.
Mine, O thou lord of life, send my roots rain.

JOHN BANISTER TABB
(1845–1909)

Christ and the Pagan

I had no God but these,
The sacerdotal Trees,
And they uplifted me.
"*I hung upon a tree.*"

The sun and moon I saw,
And reverential awe
Subdued me day and night.
"*I am the perfect light.*"

Within a lifeless Stone—
All other gods unknown—
I sought Divinity.
"*The Corner-Stone am I.*"

For sacrificial feast
I slaughtered man and beast
Red recompense to gain.
"*So I, a Lamb, was slain.*

*Yea; such My hungering Grace
That where ev'r My face
Is hidden, none may grope
Beyond eternal Hope.*"

Father Damien

O God, the cleanest offering
Of tainted earth below,
Unblushing to Thy feet we bring—
"A leper white as snow!"

JAMES JEFFREY ROCHE
(1847–1908)

The Way of the World

The hands of the king are soft and fair—
  They never knew labor's strain.
The hands of the robber redly wear
  The bloody brand of Cain.
But the hands of the Man are hard and scarred
  With the scars of toil and pain.

The slaves of Pilate have washed his hands
  As white as a king's might be.
Barabbas with wrists unfettered stands,
  For the world has made him free.
But Thy palms toil-worn by nails are torn,
  O Christ, on Calvary.

GEORGE PARSONS LATHROP
(1851–1898)

The Child's Wish Granted

Do you remember, my sweet, absent son,
How in the soft June days forever done
You loved the heavens so warm and clear and high;
And, when I lifted you, soft came your cry,—
"Put me 'way up,—'way up in the blue sky"?

I laughed and said I could not,—set you down
Your gray eyes wonder-filled beneath that crown
Of bright hair gladdening me as you raced by,
Another Father now, more strong than I,
Has borne you voiceless to your dear blue sky.

FRANCIS THOMPSON
(1859–1907)

In No Strange Land
'The Kingdom of God is within you'

O world invisible, we view thee,
O world intangible, we touch thee,
O world unknowable, we know thee,
Inapprehensible, we clutch thee!

Does the fish soar to find the ocean,
The eagle plunge to find the air—
That we ask of the stars in motion
If they have rumour of thee there?

Not where the wheeling systems darken,
And our benumb'd conceiving soars!—
The drift of pinions, would we hearken,
Beats at our own clay-shuttered doors.

The angels keep their ancient places;—
Turn but a stone and start a wing!
'Tis ye, 'tis your estrangèd faces,
That miss the many-splendoured thing.

But (when so sad thou canst not sadder)
Cry;—and upon thy so sore loss
Shall shine the traffic of Jacob's ladder
Pitched betwixt Heaven and Charing Cross.

Yea, in the night, my Soul, my daughter,
Cry,—clinging Heaven by the hems;
And lo, Christ walking on the water
Not of Gennesareth, but Thames!

ETHNA CARBERY
(1866–1902)

Mea Culpa

Be pitiful, my God!
  No hard-won gifts I bring—
But empty, pleading hands
  To Thee at evening.

Spring came, white-browed and young,
  I, too, was young with spring.
There was a blue, blue heaven
  Above a skylark's wing.

Youth is the time for joy,
  I cried, it is not meet
To mount the heights of toil
  With child-soft feet.

When Summer walked the land
  In passion's red arrayed,
Under green sweeping boughs
  My couch I made.

The noontide heat was sore,
  I slept the summer through;
An angel waked me—"Thou
  Hast work to do."

I rose and saw the sheaves
  Upstanding in a row;
The reapers sang Thy praise
  While passing to and fro.

My hands were soft with ease,
  Long were the autumn hours;
I lift the ripened sheaves
  For poppy-flowers.

But lo! now Winter glooms,
  And gray is in my hair,
Whither has flown the world
  I found so fair?

My patient God, forgive!
  Praying Thy pardon sweet
I lay a lonely heart
  Before Thy feet.

ERNEST DOWSON
(1867–1900)

Benedictio Domini

Without, the sullen noises of the street!
  The voice of London inarticulate,
Hoarse and blaspheming, surges in to meet
  The silent blessing of the Immaculate.
Dark is the church, and dim the worshippers,
  Hushed with bowed heads as though by some old spell,
While through the incense-laden air there stirs
  The admonition of a silver bell.

Dark is the church, save where the altar stands,
  Dressed like a bride, illustrious with light
Where one old priest exalts with tremulous hands
  The one true solace of man's fallen plight.
Strange silence here: without, the sounding street
  Heralds the world's swift passage to the fire;
O Benediction, perfect and complete!
  When shall men cease to suffer and desire?

Extreme Unction

Upon the eyes, the lips, the feet,
   On all the passages of sense,
The atoning oil is spread with sweet
   Renewal of lost innocence.

The feet that lately ran so fast
   To meet desire, are soothly sealed;
The eyes that were so often cast
   On vanity, are touched and healed.

From troublous sights and sounds set free
   In such a twilight hour of breath,
Shall one retrace his life or see,
   Through shadows, the true face of death?

Vials of mercy! Sacring oils!
   I know not where nor whence I come,
Nor through what wanderings and toils,
   To crave of you Viaticum.

Yet, when the walls of flesh grow weak,
   In such an hour it well may be,
Through mist and darkness, light will break,
   And each anointed sense will see.

LIONEL JOHNSON
(1867–1902)

The Dark Angel

Dark Angel, with thine aching lust
To rid the world of penitence:
Malicious Angel, who still dost
My soul such subtle violence!

Because of thee, no thought, no thing,
Abides for me undesecrate:
Dark Angel, ever on the wing,
Who never reachest me too late!

When music sounds, then changest thou
Its silvery to a sultry fire:
Nor will thine envious heart allow
Delight untortured by desire.

Through thee, the gracious Muses turn
To Furies, O mine Enemy!
And all the things of beauty burn
With flames of evil ecstasy.

Because of thee, the land of dreams
Becomes a gathering place of fears:
Until tormented slumber seems
One vehemence of useless tears.

When sunlight glows upon the flowers,
Or ripples down the dancing sea:
Thou, with thy troop of passionate powers,
Beleaguerest, bewilderest, me.

Within the breath of autumn woods,
Within the winter silences:
Thy venomous spirit stirs and broods,
O Master of impieties!

The ardor of red flame is thine,
And thine the steely soul of ice:
Thou poisonest the fair design
Of nature, with unfair device.

Apples of ashes, golden bright;
Waters of bitterness, how sweet!
O banquet of a foul delight,
Prepared by thee, dark Paraclete!

Thou art the whisper in the gloom,
The hinting tone, the haunting laugh:
Thou art the adorner of my tomb,
The minstrel of mine epitaph.

I fight thee, in the Holy Name!
Yet, what thou dost, is what God saith:
Tempter! should I escape thy flame,
Thou wilt have helped my soul from Death:

The second Death, that never dies,
That cannot die, when time is dead:
Live Death, wherein the lost soul cries,
Eternally uncomforted.

Dark Angel, with thine aching lust!
Of two defeats, of two despairs:
Less dread, a change to drifting dust,
Than thine eternity of cares.

Do what thou wilt, thou shalt not so,
Dark Angel! triumph over me:
Lonely, unto the Lone I go:
Divine, to the Divinity.

HILAIRE BELLOC
(1870–1953)

The Birds

When Jesus Christ was four years old,
The angels brought Him toys of gold,
Which no man ever had bought or sold.

And yet with these He would not play.
He made Him small fowl out of clay,
And blessed them till they flew away:
    Tu creasti Domine.

Jesus Christ, Thou child so wise,
Bless mine hands and fill mine eyes,
And bring my soul to Paradise.

Courtesy

Of Courtesy, it is much less
Than Courage of Heart or Holiness,
Yet in my Walks it seems to me
That the Grace of God is in Courtesy.

On Monks I did in Storrington fall,
They took me straight into their Hall;
I saw Three Pictures on a wall,
And Courtesy was in them all.

The first the Annunciation;
The second the Visitation;
The third the Consolation,
Of God that was Our Lady's Son.

The first was of Saint Gabriel;
On Wings a-flame from Heaven he fell;
And as he went upon one knee
He shone with Heavenly Courtesy.

Our Lady out of Nazareth rode—
It was Her month of heavy load;
Yet was Her face both great and kind,
For Courtesy was in Her Mind.

The third it was our Little Lord,
Whom all the Kings in arms adored;
He was so small you could not see
His large intent of Courtesy.

Our Lord, that was Our Lady's Son,
Go bless you, People, one by one;
My Rhyme is written, my work is done.

ROBERT HUGH BENSON
(1871–1914)

After a Retreat

What hast thou learnt to-day?
Hast thou sounded awful mysteries,
Hast pierced the veiléd skies,
Climbed to the feet of God,
Trodden where saints have trod,
Fathomed the heights above?
   Nay,
This only have I learnt, that God is love.

What hast thou heard to-day?
Hast heard the Angel-trumpets cry,
And rippling harps reply;
Heard from the Throne of flame
Whence God incarnate came
Some thund'rous message roll?
   Nay,
This have I heard, His voice within my soul.

What hast thou felt to-day?
The pinions of the Angel-guide
That standeth at thy side
In rapturous ardours beat,
Glowing, from head to feet,
In ecstasy divine?
   Nay,
This only have I felt, Christ's hand in mine.

At High Mass

Thou who hast made this world so wondrous fair;
   The pomp of clouds; the glory of the sea;
   Music of water; song-birds' melody;
The organ of Thy thunder in the air;
Breath of the rose; and beauty everywhere—
   Lord, take this stately service done to Thee,
   The grave enactment of Thy Calvary
In jewelled pomp and splendour pictured there!

Lord, take the sounds and sights; the silk and gold;
   The white and scarlet; take the reverent grace
     Of ordered step; window and glowing wall—
Prophet and Prelate, holy men of old;
   And teach us children of the Holy Place
     Who love Thy Courts, to love Thee best of all.

.

G. K. CHESTERTON
(1874–1936)

The Donkey

When fishes flew and forests walked
  And figs grew upon thorn,
Some moment when the moon was blood
  Then surely I was born.

With monstrous head and sickening cry
  And ears like errant wings,
The devil's walking parody
  On all four-footed things.

The tattered outlaw of the earth,
  Of ancient crooked will;
Starve, scourge, deride me: I am dumb,
  I keep my secret still.

Fools! For I also had my hour,
  One far fierce hour and sweet:
There was a shout about my ears,
  And palms before my feet.

The Sword of Surprise

Sunder me from my bones, O sword of God,
Till they stand stark and strange as do the trees;
That I whose heart goes up with the soaring woods
May marvel as much at these.

Sunder me from my blood that in the dark
I hear that red ancestral river run,
Like branching buried floods that find the sea
But never see the sun.

Give me miraculous eyes to see my eyes,
Those rolling mirrors made alive in me,
Terrible crystal more incredible
Than all the things they see.

Sunder me from my soul, that I may see
The sins like streaming wounds, the life's brave beat;
Till I shall save myself, as I would save
A stranger in the street.

The Great Minimum

It is something to have wept as we have wept,
It is something to have done as we have done,
It is something to have watched as when all men slept,
And seen the stars which never see the sun.

It is something to have smelt the mystic rose,
Although it break and leave the thorny rods,
It is something to have hungered once as those
Must hunger who have ate the bread of gods.

To have seen you and your unforgotten face,
Brave as a blast of trumpets for the fray,
Pure as white lilies in a watery space,
It were something, though you went from me to-day.

To have known the things that from the weak are furled,
Perilous ancient passions, strange and high;
It is something to be wiser than the world,
It is something to be older than the sky.

In a time of sceptic moths and cynic rusts,
And fatted lives that of their sweetness tire,
In a world of flying loves and fading lusts,
It is something to be sure of a desire.

Lo, blessed are our ears for they have heard;
Yea, blessed are our eyes for they have seen:
Let thunder break on man and beast and bird
And the lightning. It is something to have been.

RAINER MARIA RILKE
(1875–1926)

Autumn

The leaves are falling, falling as from way off,
as though far gardens withered in the skies;
they are falling with denying gestures.

And in the nights the heavy earth is falling
from all the stars down into loneliness.

We all are falling. This hand falls.
And look at others: it is in them all.

And yet there is one who holds this falling
endlessly gently in his hands.

JOYCE KILMER
(1886–1918)

The Robe of Christ

At the foot of the Cross on Calvary
   Three soldiers sat and diced,
And one of them was the Devil
   And he won the Robe of Christ.

When the Devil comes in his proper form
   To the chamber where I dwell,
I know him and make the Sign of the Cross
   Which drives him back to Hell.

And when he comes like a friendly man
   And puts his hand in mine,
The fervour in his voice is not
   From love or joy or wine.

And when he comes like a woman,
   With lovely, smiling eyes,
Black dreams float over his golden head
   Like a swarm of carrion flies.

Now many a million tortured souls
   In his red halls there be:
Why does he spend his subtle craft
   In hunting after me?

Kings, queens and crested warriors
   Whose memory rings through time,
These are his prey, and what to him
   Is this poor man of rhyme,

That he, with such laborious skill,
   Should change from rôle to rôle,
Should daily act so many a part
   To get my little soul?

Oh, he can be the forest,
   And he can be the sun,
Or a buttercup, or an hour of rest
   When the weary day is done.

I saw him through a thousand veils,
   And has not this sufficed?
Now, must I look on the Devil robed
   In the radiant Robe of Christ?

He comes, and his face is sad and mild,
   With thorns his head is crowned;
There are great bleeding wounds in his feet,
   And in each hand a wound.

How can I tell, who am a fool,
   If this be Christ or no?
Those bleeding hands outstretched to me!
   Those eyes that love me so!

I see the Robe—I look—I hope—
   I fear—but there is one
Who will direct my troubled mind;
   Christ's Mother knows her Son.

O Mother of Good Counsel, lend
    Intelligence to me!
Encompass me with wisdom,
    Thou Tower of Ivory!

"This is the Man of Lies," she says,
    "Disguised with fearful art:
He has the wounded hands and feet,
    But not the wounded heart."

Besides the Cross on Calvary
    She watched them as they diced.
She saw the Devil join the game
    And win the Robe of Christ.

JOSEPH MARY PLUNKETT
(1887–1916)

I See His Blood upon the Rose

I see His blood upon the rose
    And in the stars the glory of His eyes,
His Body gleams amid eternal snows,
    His tears fall from the skies.

I see His face in every flower;
    The thunder and the singing of the birds
Are but His voice—and carven by His power
    Rocks are His written words.

All pathways by His feet are worn,
    His strong heart stirs the ever-beating sea,
His crown of thorns is twined with every thorn,
    His Cross is every tree.

T. S. ELIOT
(1888–1965)

Journey of the Magi

'A cold coming we had of it,
Just the worst time of the year
For a journey, and such a long journey:
The ways deep and the weather sharp,
The very dead of winter.'
And the camels galled, sore-footed, refractory,
Lying down in the melting snow.
There were times we regretted
The summer palaces on slopes, the terraces,
And the silken girls bringing sherbet.
Then the camel men cursing and grumbling
And running away, and wanting their liquor and women,
And the night-fires going out, and the lack of shelters,
And the cities hostile and the towns unfriendly
And the villages dirty and charging high prices:
A hard time we had of it.
At the end we preferred to travel all night,
Sleeping in snatches,
With the voices singing in our ears, saying
That this was all folly.

Then at dawn we came down to a temperate valley,
Wet, below the snow line, smelling of vegetation;
With a running stream and a water-mill beating the
     darkness,
And three trees on the low sky,
And an old white horse galloped away in the meadow.
Then we came to a tavern with vine-leaves over the
     lintel,
Six hands at an open door dicing for pieces of silver,
And feet kicking the empty wine-skins.

But there was no information, and so we continued
And arrived at evening, not a moment too soon
Finding the place; it was (you may say) satisfactory.

All this was a long time ago, I remember,
And I would do it again, but set down
This set down
This: were we led all that way for
Birth or Death? There was a Birth, certainly,
We had evidence and no doubt. I had seen birth and
     death,
But had thought they were different; this Birth was
Hard and bitter agony for us, like Death, our death.
We returned to our places, these Kingdoms,
But no longer at ease here, in the old dispensation,
With an alien people clutching their gods.
I should be glad of another death.

EDNA ST. VINCENT MILLAY
(1892–1950)

God's World

O world, I cannot hold thee close enough!
   Thy winds, thy wide grey skies!
   Thy mists, that roll and rise!
Thy woods, this autumn day, that ache and sag
And all but cry with colour! That gaunt crag
To crush! To lift the lean of that black bluff!
World, World, I cannot get thee close enough!

Long have I known a glory in it all,
    But never knew I this:
    Here such a passion is
As stretcheth me apart,—Lord, I do fear
Thou'st made the world too beautiful this year;
My soul is all but out of me,—let fall
No burning leaf; prithee, let no bird call.

LEONARD FEENEY
(1897–1978)

I Burned My Bridges

I burned my bridges when I had crossed.
I never brooded on what I lost,
Nor ruined with rapine my holocaust.

Youth is a rapture we must forget;
Wither and wrinkle without regret.
Hobble to Heaven and do not fret.

Yet in my soul there is something still
Deeper than memory, mind and will,
Something alive that I cannot kill.

Part of me, put not in my keeping,
Awakes unawakened when I am sleeping,
Under my laughter it goes on weeping

For by-gone beaches and limbs of brown,
When hoops were rolling around the town,
And London Bridges were falling down.

The Way of the Cross

Along the dark aisles
  Of a chapel dim,
The little lame girl
  Drags her withered limb.
And all alone she searches
  The shadows on the walls,
To find the three pictures
  Where Jesus falls.

Nails

Whenever the bright blue nails would drop
Down on the floor of his carpenter shop,
Saint Joseph, prince of carpenter men,
Would stoop to gather them up again;
For he feared for two little sandals sweet,
And very easy to pierce they were
As they pattered over the lumber there
And rode on two little sacred feet.

But alas, on a hill between earth and heaven
One day two nails in a cross were driven,
And fastened it firm to the sacred feet
Where once rode two little sandals sweet;
And Christ and His mother looked off in death
Afar—to the valley of Nazareth,
Where the carpenter's shop was spread with dust
And the little blue nails, all packed in rust,
Slept in a box on the window-sill;
And Joseph lay sleeping under the hill.

Resurrection

In crocus fashion, sunlight-wise,
   The body of Our Lord
Slipped through the stone-bound sepulchre,
   Streamed through the soldier's sword.

Though stripped and whipped and spat upon,
   Sundered by nail and spear,
Thus did our dust in Him prevail
   At the robin-time of the year.

Albeit our interval under earth
   Must needs much longer last,
Let there be always ready the roll
   Of drums and the trumpet blast.

With bones ablaze and flesh aflash
   And hair set flying free,
So shall I come to you, loved ones,
   So shall you come to me.

ROY CAMPBELL
(1901–1957)

Mass at Dawn

I dropped my sail and dried my dripping seines
Where the white quay is chequered by cool planes
In whose great branches, always out of sight,
The nightingales are singing day and night.
Though all was grey beneath the moon's grey beam,
My boat in her new paint shone like a bride,
And silver in my baskets shone the bream:
My arms were tired and I was heavy-eyed,
But when with food and drink, at morning-light,
The children met me at the water-side,
Never was wine so red or bread so white.

Toledo, July 1936

Toledo, when I saw you die
And heard the roof of Carmel crash,
A spread-winged phoenix from its ash
The Cross remained against the sky!
With horns of flame and haggard eye
The mountain vomited with blood,
A thousand corpses down the flood
Were rolled gesticulating by,
And high above the roaring shells
I heard the silence of your bells
Who've left these broken stones behind
Above the years to make your home,
And burn, with Athens and with Rome,
A sacred city of the mind.

PHYLLIS McGINLEY
(1905–1978)

Sonnet from Assisi

Blind Francis, waiting to welcome Sister Death,
Worn though he was by ecstasies and fame,
Had heart for tune. With what remained of breath
He led his friars in canticles.

                Then came
Brother Elias, scowling, to his side,
Small-souled Elias, crying by book and candle,
This was outrageous! Had the monks no pride?
Music at deathbeds! Ah, the shame, the scandal!

Elias gave him sermons and advice
Instead of song; which simply proves once more
What things are sure this side of paradise:
Death, taxes, and the counsel of the bore.
Though we outwit the tithe, make death our friend,
Bores we have with us even to the end.

Paterfamilias

Of all the saints who have won their charter—
Holy man, hero, hermit, martyr,
Mystic, missioner, sage, or wit—
Saint Thomas More is my favorite.

For he loved these bounties with might and main:
God and his house and his little wife, Jane,
And four fair children his heart throve on,
Margaret, Elizabeth, Cecily, and John.

That More was a good man everybody knows.
He sang good verses and he wrote good prose,
Enjoyed a good caper and liked a good meal
And made a good Master of the Privy Seal.
A friend to Erasmus, Lily's friend,
He lived a good life and he had a good end
And left good counsel for them to con,
Margaret, Elizabeth, Cecily, and John.

Some saints are alien, hard to love,
Wild as an eagle, strange as a dove,
Too near to heaven for the mind to scan.
But Thomas More was a family man,
A husband, a courtier, a doer, and a hoper
(Admired of his son-in-law, Mr. Roper),
Who punned in Latin like a Cambridge don
With Margaret, Elizabeth, Cecily, and John.

R. S. THOMAS
(1913–2000)

The Country Clergy

I see them working in old rectories
By the sun's light, by candlelight,
Venerable men, their black cloth
A little dusty, a little green
With holy mildew. And yet their skulls,
Ripening over so many prayers,
Toppled into the same grave
With oafs and yokels. They left no books,
Memorial to their lonely thought
In grey parishes; rather they wrote
On men's hearts and in the minds
Of young children sublime words
Too soon forgotten. God in his time
Or out of time will correct this.

Ann Griffith

So God spoke to her,
she the poor girl from the village
without learning. 'Play me,'
he said, 'on the white keys
of your body. I have seen you dance
for the bridegrooms that were not
to be, while I waited for you
under the ripening boughs of
the myrtle. These people know me
only in the thin hymns of
the mind, in the arid sermons
and prayers. I am the live God,
nailed fast to the old tree
of a nation by its unreal
tears. I thirst, I thirst
for the spring water. Draw it up
for me from your heart's well and I will change
it to wine upon your unkissed lips.'

KAROL WOJTYLA
(Pope John Paul II)
(1920–)

Her Amazement at Her Only Child

Light piercing, gradually, everyday events;
a woman's eyes, hands
used to them since childhood.
Then brightness flared, too huge for simple days,
and hands clasped when the words lost their space.

In that little town, my son, where they knew us together,
you called me mother; but no one had eyes to see
the astounding events as they took place day by day.
Your life became the life of the poor
in your wish to be with them through the work of your
     hands.

I knew: the light that lingered in ordinary things,
like a spark sheltered under the skin of our days—
the light was you;
it did not come from me.

And I had more of you in that luminous silence
than I had of you as the fruit of my body, my blood.

JOHN GILLESPIE MAGEE, JR.
(1922–1941)

High Flight

Oh, I have slipped the surly bonds of earth,
And danced the skies on laughter-silvered wings;
Sunward I've climbed and joined the tumbling mirth
Of sun-split clouds—and done a hundred things
You have not dreamed of—wheeled and soared and
    swung
High in the sunlit silence. Hov'ring there,
I've chased the shouting wind along and flung
My eager craft through footless halls of air.
Up, up the long delirious burning blue
I've topped the wind-swept heights with easy grace,
Where never lark, or even eagle, flew;
And, while with silent, lifting mind I've trod
The high untrespassed sanctity of space,
Put out my hand, and touched the face of God.

JOHN SENIOR
(1923–1998)

A Song

My father died upon a tree,
my mother's in the ground:
Oh bury me most merrily,
and dance my grave around!

The sheep are in the hills above,
the shepherd's in the hay,
I sing my merry songs of love,
upon my pipe I play.

The wind blows down the valleys wild,
the woods have lost their way!
I sing because a pretty Child
was born on Christmas Day.

Lauds

Praise death,
that Sahara,
barren as Sarah
and Elizabeth.

AIDAN MULLANEY
(1925–)

On the Night of Hugo

In the darkness of that night—
That darkness on every side of me,
Above, around and within me—
In that darkness that brought uprooting
And pruning so far beyond the wildest
Images I had known,
In that darkness I sought You, Lord,
And You came
Not in any way I could foreknow
Nor in a way I could imagine.

You found me, Lord,
In my knowledge of my nothingness.

In that nothingness, my Lord,
Now am I content to be
For now I can perceive
That Your Love has ever sheltered me
From grievous harms on every side of me
In every place, in every time.

It is this perceiving, Lord, that
Now impels me seeking, ever searching
Ever thirsting, longing, yearning
For that Center that is
Thine own most gracious Heart
Beyond all space and time.

JOHANN MOSER
(1940-)

Bordeaux, 408 A.D.
(*in two voices*)

"At anchor in the harbor, now,
   Galleys of the western fleet prepare to sail.
The sun rides low beyond the ocean;
   On our table, a cruet of Burdigalan wine
Glows fiery-red in evening light,
   And we watch the somber nightfall
      Lean its brow upon the sea."

"Should we not prepare to leave as well?"

     "Where would we go?
The Augustan legions are withdrawn;
     The Rhine frontier has fallen.
Like bats in a gutted tower,
     The *foederati* flutter through the empire
Seeking a blackened perch amid the ruins.
     And Alaric turns his raven's eye
Down the Flaminian viaducts,
   Down to the Alban Hills, and—dare I say it?—
'The walls of lofty Rome.'
     The stays of the imperium cannot hold."

"But the matter of perpetuity!"

"Ah, we can but cherish what has been bestowed;
We can but praise what lived before us,
    And will yield its gracious foison to the ages.
Perpetuity renders us,
        But is not ours to render; all human excellence
Alone is quarried in the hands of God.
        But look, upon the darkening waves,
The galleys trim their starboard lamps."

    "When will they depart?"

"They sail with the tide, those ships;
            They will not come again.
Lucinius has joined them.
        He stuffed his earthen jars with scraps:
Souvenirs of the old campaigns—
    A battered eagle or two, medallions from Trier.
What does it matter? He sails for Spain.
        The *barbaroi* will be there to meet him.
Shall he embark for Africa?
    Numidian grain-fields shall be red with blood
Before he unpacks his wares."

    "And us?"

                ". . . compose the hymns
Which they at morning will intone
        To laud the new-born sun, the ancient land,
The same ripened apples
            Loaded into carts at harvest-time.
Someday they too shall walk these hills
        And take the poplars for their song
And sing a lady's beauty.
    Someday they too shall aptly raise
Basilicas of thought into the heavens."

          "Until then . . . ?"
"Until then . . . ?
    The wine, my friend, a final cup;
The night is growing heavy,
        And I must homeward bend my way
To stave my lids, my weary soul,
    Against that long-encroaching,
            That dark and ageless sea.
May Roman peace betide us
            Among the solemn groves,
The sepulchres of our fathers in their sleep."

TIMOTHY J. WILLIAMS
(1957–)

Doubters

The Feast at Cana is comic stuff
for doubters having learned enough
to reserve their reliance
for the "miracles" of science.
(And the slow miracle of yeast and vine
transforming showers into wine?)

Others scoff at the Body made from wheat
—"Hocus-pocus!" they repeat.
(Nonetheless, their daily bread
at last
joins fast
to heart, hand, and head.)

Others still with tankards join,
bemused at what their wits will coin:
"I'll be damned," they say,
"if wine turns Blood that way!"
(And as ever more they drink,
ever less substantial is what they think—
the cause being this very flood
of good wine turning vintage blood.)

∼

What Nature works upon slowly
her Author quickens for the lowly
to speed the salvation of these humble,
though it cause the proud to stumble.

Reconciliation

Mary, Mother,
See this child!
—Still another
Reconciled
Who was tossed
Without the Ark,
Was feared lost
In gathering dark,
By rising waters
Nearly drowned,
Yet merely washed
And newly found.

Oh, that we may see
The end of sin!
Do keep us free,
Virgin Blessed,
Eternally
From things confessed.
By the Son
You hold so dear
Be undone
Our mortal fear
And calmed the sea
That swells within.
Oh, pray your Son
His Spirit send
To steer our ship
Unto its End.

AMANDA GLASS
(1977–)

Mors in Auroram

When birds begin their morning-song
and light puts dark to flight,
oh, give me then a requiem
to start my day out right!

Do not assault my ears with cheer
which bright new mornings bring.
But let me dwell on fear and death,
and wake to Four Last Things!

All Souls' Day Lament

As slate clouds rush across a diamond sky
and trees disintegrate in splendid shreds
and the sleep of the chilly earth breathes forth—I
stand at the center, sunk in awe and dread
of the pressing primal powers sweeping the world
with screaming speed, ramping furious and free
like some massive creature, tent-like wings unfurled,
beating air in destructive glory and glee.

In searing contrast, there exists in me
a silent static deep, so paralyzed,
so sunk in pseudo-death, that when I see
one from damning torpor exorcised,
I could weep. Suffer me to be battered in the storm;
scorch my soul to save its fragile form.

Acknowledgments

The compiler and the publisher gratefully acknowledge the following for permission to reprint poems included in this book.

A P Watt Ltd., for "The Donkey", "The Sword of Surprise", and "The Great Minimum", by G. K. Chesterton. Reprinted by permission of A P Watt Ltd. on behalf of The Royal Literary Fund. These poems were taken from *The Collected Poems of G. K. Chesterton*. New York: Dodd, Mead and Company, 1980.

Elizabeth Barnett, for "God's World", by Edna St. Vincent Millay. Reprinted by permission of Elizabeth Barnett, Literary Executor.

Amanda Glass, for permission to reprint "Mors in Auroram" and "All Soul's Day Lament".

Harcourt, Inc. for "Journey of the Magi", by T. S. Eliot. "Journey of the Magi" from *Collected Poems, 1909–1962*, by T. S. Eliot. Copyright © 1936 by Harcourt, Inc. Copyright © 1964, 1963 by T. S. Eliot. Reprinted by permission of the publisher.

Hillsdale College, for "A Song" and "Lauds", by John Senior. Reprinted by permission of Dr. David M. Whalen, Hillsdale College.

Father Aidan Mullaney, for permission to reprint "On the Night of Hugo".

Penguin Putnam Inc. for "Paterfamilias" and "Sonnet from Assisi" by Phyllis McGinley. "Paterfamilias",

The compiler and the publisher are grateful to all the poets and publishers whose work is represented in this book.

Index of Authors

Index of Titles

Index of First Lines